The Sunflo
That Went F

Suitable for making into a blown-up book for shared reading.

Mrs Brown
had a sunflower
growing by the wall.

It was straight and tall,
and yellow as the sun.

The people passing by
looked at it and said,
"What a beauty!"

Day after day,
the sunflower stood tall,
by the wall,
under the hot sun.

Then, one afternoon,
suddenly,
the sunflower
went
FLOP.

"What a shame!"
said the people passing by.

"Oh, my poor flower,"
cried Mrs Brown.
And she ran to Mr Brown.

"What is it, my love?" he asked.

"Our big yellow sunflower went FLOP," she said.

Mr Brown only laughed.
"Don't get in a tizz," he said.
"I'll fix it.
I can fix anything."

Mr Brown opened up his fix-it bag,
and got out some sticky tape.
"This should do it," he said.

He went stick, stick, stick,
and stood the sunflower
up by the wall again.

"What a clever man
you are," said Mrs Brown.

Mr Brown put away
his fix-it bag.
"Think nothing of it,
my love," he said.
"It was easy."

The sun was hot all day,
and the next afternoon,
suddenly,
the sunflower
went
FLOP.

"What a shame!"
said the people passing by.

Mrs Brown saw it and cried,
"My poor sunflower!"
And she called Mr Brown.

"What is it, my love?" he asked.

"Our sunflower went FLOP again,"
she said.

Mr Brown only laughed.
"Don't get in a tizz," he said.
"I'll fix it.
I can fix anything."

He opened his fix-it bag,
and got out
a needle and string.

"This should do it,"
he said.
He went stitch, stitch, stitch,
and stitched the sunflower
up by the wall.

"What a clever man you are,"
said Mrs Brown.

Mr Brown put away
his fix-it bag.

"Think nothing of it, my love,"
he said.
"It was easy."

The sun was hot
all day,
and the next afternoon,
suddenly,
the sunflower
went
FLOP.

"What a shame!"
said the people passing by.

"Oh dear, oh dear,"
cried Mrs Brown.

"What is it, my love?"
said Mr Brown.

"Our sunflower has gone FLOP again,"
said Mrs Brown.

Mr Brown only laughed.
"Don't get in a tizz," he said.
"I'll fix it. I can fix anything."

He opened up his fix-it bag,
and got out a hammer and nails.
"This should do it," he said.

He went hammer, hammer, hammer,
and stood the sunflower
up by the wall again.

"What a clever man you are,"
said Mrs Brown.

Mr Brown put away his fix-it bag.
"Think nothing of it, my love,"
he said. "It was easy."

The sun was hot all day,
and the next afternoon,
suddenly,
the sunflower
went
FLOP.

"What a shame!"
said the people passing by.

Mrs Brown looked at it
and shook her head.
Then she went to tell Mr Brown.
"It's done it again," she said.

"Oh," said Mr Brown.
"Blow!" said Mr Brown.

"Can you fix it?"
asked Mrs Brown.

"Of course," said Mr Brown.
"I can fix anything.
But let's do it in the morning.
I'm always best at fixing things
in the morning."

That night,
it rained
and rained
and rained.

The sunflower
drank
and drank
and drank.

It grew
straight and tall
again.

The next morning,
the people passing by
stopped to look.
"What a beauty!" they said.

Mrs Brown
went to the window.
"My sunflower!" she cried.

Then she ran to Mr Brown
and hugged him.
"I don't know how you did it," she said.
"You fixed it. You really fixed it.
What a *clever* man you are."

But Mr Brown only laughed.
"Think nothing of it, my love," he said.
"It was easy."